The *Why I Write* series is
published with assistance from
the Windham-Campbell
Literature Prizes, which are
administered by the Beinecke
Rare Book and Manuscript
Library at Yale University.

Yale University Press books may be
purchased in quantity for educational,
business, or promotional use.
For information, please e-mail
sales.press@yale.edu (U.S. office) or
sales@yaleup.co.uk (U.K. office).

Printed in the United States
of America.

Library of Congress Control
Number: 2018940022
ISBN 978-0-300-22151-0
(hardcover : alk. paper)

A catalogue record for this book is
available from the British Library.

This paper meets the requirements
of ANSI/NISO Z39.48-1992
(Permanence of Paper).

10 9 8 7 6 5 4 3 2 1

INADVERTENT

The question of why I write sounds simple, but simplicity is treacherous, for now I have been sitting here in front of my desk in southern Sweden for three days without making any headway. The first thing that came to mind was a television interview with an author that I saw many years ago; he walked into the studio saying, "I write because I am going to die." He had clearly thought about it for a long time, and perhaps he even meant it, but he had tucked his sweater into his trousers, and the contrast between the solemnity of his words and his bungling manner of dress made it hard to take him seriously. I laughed at him, I remember, but now, sitting here faced with the same task as he had been, I understand how difficult it is.

Why did I laugh, when not only did his response clearly spring from a deep conviction but was one I could actually relate to, if not quite subscribe to?

It was the incongruity between his words and the context in which they were spoken that was comical, that his sweater was tucked into his trousers created a distance to what he said, and the chasm separating death's solemnity from life's unceremoniousness became apparent. This distance is literary, it is precisely that space literature explores, between something that is true and the setting in which truth unfolds. It is the space of Don Quixote, which plays out in the distance between what he imagines he is seeing and the world as it is, and it is the space of Madame Bovary, shaped by the distance between what she wishes the world were like and how it actually is.

Literature is not primarily a place for truths, it is the space where truths play out. For the answer to the question — that I write because I am going to die — to have the intended effect, for it to strike one as truth, a space must first be created in which it can be said. That is what writing is: creating a space in which something can be said.

Some years ago I wrote a book about the Norwegian painter Edvard Munch. It dealt primarily with space, naturally enough, given that the theme was visual art, and perhaps Edvard Munch's greatest achievement was that he closed up the realistic pictorial space which dominated painting when he was growing up, first and foremost in his youthful work *The Sick Child* but also in paintings such as *The Scream* and *Ashes*. Realistic pictorial space is stable, it obeys the same rules of depiction regardless of what happens in it, and in this continuity, which allows for a before and an after, there lies the possibility of reconciliation. In *The Sick Child* the space is closed, or powerfully distorted, and in *The Scream* the entire space is subsumed into the face and the state of mind it expresses. We cannot evade what is happening in these pictures; death in the former and anxiety in the latter are acutely present, there is no distance to be had, we are defenseless against them.

The question I posed was why only Munch chose to go in that direction and paint that way, and not any of the other young painters who were active in Kristiania (later Oslo) at the time, many of whom were clearly more talented than Munch. There must have been some incongruity between his experience of reality and the dominant way of depicting it, an incongruity so great that he couldn't simply accept the existing painterly idiom if he wanted to be true to himself, but had to fight against it, working his way blindly inward, and not give up until he had brought out something external that corresponded with his inner experience. He spent more than a year painting *The Sick Child*, the picture that marked the turning point, and it looks as if it had been *dug up*.

Everyone who has attempted to paint knows that it is a painstaking and complicated process, governed by a special form of thought, visual and unreflecting, almost like the colors and shapes themselves. It takes many years to acquire enough experience and confidence to be able to express what one wants on the canvas, or at least to minimize the distance between the internal and the external image so that the visual and unreflecting thoughts can move more or less freely between their inner and outer expression. The medium is physical, the picture is an object in the world made up of oil paints and canvas, and if it had been possible to stand next to Edvard Munch on a summer day in for example 1896, while he stood painting outside his house in Aasgaardstrand, for example some girls on a pier with a few houses and trees in the background, it is hard to imagine that he would look up, push his hat back on his head, and say, "I'm really doing this because I have lost trust in the world," then anything other than this, and he is beautiful, with a large, sensitive mouth and nervous eyes, large, restless hands. At the same time he is arrogant, a self-important and haughty man from a family of famous academics, and he drinks nearly every night, in the pale summer nights which are so quiet that his voice and those of his friends carry a long way in the residential streets and out across the still fjord. Later in life he secludes himself, cuts out friends and lovers, grows tetchy and impossible, an unreasonable old man who, when he meets someone, talks incessantly about everything and nothing, it's impossible to get a word in edgewise once he gets going. Whereas when he was young, at least during a short ten-year period, he painted scenes from his own life, memories he had, for the remainder of his life he painted what he saw in front of him. Houses, plains, tractors, horses, laborers, trees, people, his own face. He lived a long life, from the middle of the nineteenth century and into the Second World War, and he painted throughout it all. One of his last pictures depicts a housepainter who painted the buildings on his estate, and it is as if he is saying, this is what I too do and have spent my whole life doing, brushing paint onto a surface. But the sun is shining, the house is white, and deep within the green of the garden a red barn wall is glowing.

Could a lack of trust in the world really have driven him to paint one thousand seven hundred pictures and produce more than twenty thousand prints, could it have been the driving force behind his entire long life with all its victories and defeats?

If the distance is great enough, the answer is yes — seen from a great distance, a life can be summed up in a single sentence — but as soon as one comes closer to life, it dissolves into an ocean of time, events, things, and people. It is still there, somewhere in the multitude, but it is no longer supreme, for in a life seen at close range there is no organizing principle.

We live in an ocean of time, where events, things, and people are continually succeeding one another, but we cannot live with such boundless complexity, because we disappear in it, and therefore we organize it into categories, sequences, hierarchies. We organize ourselves—I am not nameless, my name is such and such, my parents were like this and that, I went to school in such and such a place, I experienced this and that, by character I am like this and like that, and that has caused me to choose this and that. And we organize our surroundings—we don't just live on a plain with some grass, bushes, roads, and houses, we live in a particular place in a particular country with a particular culture, and we belong to a particular stratum within that culture.

All of us sum up our lives in this way, that is what we call identity; and we sum up the world we inhabit in similar ways, that is what is called culture. What we are saying about ourselves fits, but no more than if we had said something entirely different, thought something entirely different about ourselves and our place in the world — if, for example, we had lived during the Middle Ages and not in the early twenty-first century — and it too would have fit and seemed meaningful.

That identity and our understanding of the world at one and the same time fit yet are arbitrary is, I think, the reason why art and literature exist. Art and literature constitute a continual negotiation with reality, they represent an exchange between identity and culture and the material, physical, and endlessly complex world they arise from.

But that isn't why I write. Nor was it why Munch painted. For the negotiation is always personal, never — or extremely rarely — ideational or representative.

If this is my understanding of art and life, why did I simplify so crudely and write that Munch painted because he had lost trust in the world?

There are some fundamental rules of writing, for example that one shouldn't psychologize when describing characters, or the related dictum "Show, don't tell," both of which spring from the realization that literature by its very nature always seeks complexity and ambiguity, and that monologic claims of truth about the world are antiliterary. In line with this, the statement "I write because I am going to die" is antiliterature, but the author with his sweater tucked into his trousers saying that he writes because he is going to die is literature.

For many years I followed these rules of writing, that one shouldn't psychologize and that one shouldn't tell, but show. However, the texts I wrote ended up being neither complex nor ambiguous; on the contrary they were closed and unfree, as if the space they unfolded in was a prison, with locked doors and no windows. It wasn't until I started breaking the rules, showing how something was and should be understood, very precisely and with no room for doubt, and describing people in psychological terms, that my writing came alive. This was so, I think, because even in the most meticulous and exhaustive explanation of a person's character or actions, even in the most heavy-handed explication, there is always an outside. Language and literary form themselves contain a distance, making it impossible ever to get all the way in or to eliminate space entirely. All language casts a shadow, and that shadow can be more or less apprehended, but never quite controlled.

The first novel I wrote is full of sentences such as "It's like this" and "That's how it is." The first-person narrator—who incidentally is not at all unlike myself—had a problem with authority and authoritarianism, he was strongly opposed to it, but at the same time he needed it, for his life was adrift, it was full of uncertainty, hesitation, inability to act, and that conflict, which was fundamental, not only made necessary the categorical claims about the world and the people in it, it also under-mined them completely – revealing a person who is using them to keep his head above water. The statements themselves are not nec-essarily untrue, but the space around them rel-ativizes them utterly. When I wrote the novel, I didn't know this, the confident claims about the world were probably as necessary to me as they were to my protagonist. If I had thought out this pattern beforehand, used it as a strat-egy, it would have become totally unbearable to the reader, for then there would have been no space around it, it would have been mono-logic and unambiguous, it would have lacked the sweater tucked into the trousers. It wasn't until I discovered this, that the distance of form and language created a space into which I could pour my self, where I lost ownership and con-trol over it and where what was me was trans-formed into "me," that I became a writer.

That wasn't why I began writing, since for a long time I didn't know this, yet I still wrote.

"Mommy, the comics man is here!" I remember my greed, my simple and almost trembling joy at the sheer numbers, for a big pile of comics I hadn't read before meant hours, maybe days in bed under the spell of these stories. But this life of abundance ended abruptly when one day my mother began to take an interest in what I was reading. She was shaken to the core. Many of the comic series were violent and sexist, and I was just nine years old. Besides, her sister had written her master's thesis in psychology on violence in comic books, so she was already on her guard against brutalizing tendencies. She said I wasn't allowed to read comics anymore. I cried, the punishment was incomprehensible, I hadn't done anything wrong! But, she said, you're allowed to read books. I'll take you and your brother to the library every Tuesday. It wasn't the same, but at least it was something, so I came with her, sitting in the green Volkswagen Beetle as we crossed the bridge, drove along the sound and into town, where about and read over and over again through-out my childhood and into my teens. The book was called *A Wizard of Earthsea* and was writ-ten by Ursula K. Le Guin. It was my mother who brought it for me one day, she was study-ing that year and came home only on weekends. It was winter, swollen mounds of snow lay everywhere, and that Friday I was longing so intensely for her to come home that I couldn't stay in my room, but went out in the hope of running into someone I could play with. I remember hardly anything from that year, but this I do remember, that I am walking down the deserted hill outside the house and lie down on a mound of snow and move my arms back and forth to make an angel in the snow. Afterward I lie still for a long time, gazing up into the dark-ness. The feeling of the cold rising from the snow and the vague but still unmistakable smell of snow and the sound of the smooth mate-rial of my down jacket against the snow made something lift within me. Shortly afterward a car came driving up the hill, its sound muted by the snow, which shone yellow in the headlights. There was no mistaking the sound, it was her car, she was finally here. I ran over to the car as she was parking outside the house and walked to the front door with her. She said she had a present for me, and it was that book, which I got when we had taken off our outer clothes; it lay in her handbag with no wrapping paper around it.

It's strange how the event one remembers attaches itself to the moments surrounding it, which without it would have been lost, since they don't contain anything memorable. Yet those are the moments we live our lives in, while those we remember, which we construct our identities around, are often the exceptions. That is why what Proust called involuntary memories are so powerful – what a smell, such as that of wet asphalt on a foggy autumn evening, or a taste, such as that of cold boiled mackerel and a cucumber slice soaked in vinegar, can reawaken is completely unprocessed, time appears in an almost raw state, beyond the control of thought and memory, connected with life as it was actually lived. For me as for most people, the primary catalyst for this kind of memory is music. During this particular period, on those particular nights, I was listening to Wings and their album *Back to the Egg*. I still occasionally play that album now, not because it's so good but because that particular time is encapsulated in it, and especially *A Wizard of Earthsea:* the atmosphere of that book, that music, and that period of my life are inextricably interwoven within me. And I think that what that mood represented, the place it created within me, is one of the most important reasons that I later began to write. I wanted to enter that space again.

But what kind of a book is it, which not only left a deep mark on me but also gathers around itself a wreath of memories from an otherwise memoryless time?

A Wizard of Earthsea is a fairy tale. It is set in a world of islands and seas, during premodern times; people travel by horse and by ship. There are wizards there, so magic is possible, but not for everyone. Every thing, every animal, and every human being has a true name, outside of language, linked to what it really is. The art of magic is connected with these names: if one knows the name one can control the thing, the animal, the person. The protagonist is a boy named Ged; he is from an outlying region, he is gifted but proud and ambitious, he impatiently seeks recognition, and when his skills are discovered and he is admitted to a school of wizardry, his boasting and self-assertiveness drive him to cross the border into the land of the dead, to prove his worth to the others. He almost dies, falls into a coma and barely pulls through, but a creature, a kind of spirit or demon, enters the world because of this. He senses its coldness, hides from it, flees from it, farther and farther away, and knows that he cannot become free of it until he has come to know its true name. Toward the end of the book, when the spirit has come very near and intends either to take Ged over or to destroy him, he suddenly realizes that it bears his own name.

It may seem infantile to bring up a children's book in an essay about why I write, a regressive elevation of something that might have an effect on a ten-year-old, but which has no value in adult life, other than as nostalgia, or in other words, a form of homesickness.

Why don't I write instead about the influence of *Ulysses*, whose virtually inexhaustible insights and praxises may suffice for an entire long life of writing? Or about Anne Carson's poems or Vanessa Baird's pictures, both of which open up mythological space in present time to dizzying effect, in ways as true as they are unfathomable?

A Wizard of Earthsea is a children's book, but the feelings it evoked in me are not exclusive to childhood, for unlike our thoughts, our emotions do not change in the course of a life, at least not in a fundamental way: joy is the same to a ten-year-old as to a seventy-year-old, as are grief, anger, jealousy, loathing, and enthusiasm. All the books I read as a child brought out feelings in me, but they dealt with a world out there, which I left as soon as I closed the covers. This book related to feelings that concerned me, the person I was and the world I lived in. It opened the way for a kind of unreflecting, emotion-driven thoughts, something I had never experienced before; they were new to me and almost shockingly powerful.

I didn't know that I had a strong need to be seen, I didn't know that such a thing as a desire to be seen even existed at all. That everything I did came to have a life beyond me, essentially other than the person I was, yet still inexorably tied to me, this I had already experienced, but I had never thought about it, it remained unarticulated within me. Reading didn't articulate it for me, it didn't make me start thinking about it, but it let me feel it. It gave my feelings a form and a direction. It was an awakening, but it took place, as it were, inside a book, and even though it was painful, it also felt good, perhaps precisely because it didn't have any external consequences but remained inside me.

This emotion-based way of thinking and understanding is unique to literature, or to certain kinds of literature, and although I lost sight of it for many years, while I was studying literature and literary theory and believed that only the cerebral had any value, that insight could be gained only through reflection, it never left me — I read *Ulysses* and admired it tremendously, but it was "The Dead" that really left a mark on me, and when I read Dostoevsky's *The Idiot* it wasn't my thought that was set alight but my feelings.

Thoughts and feelings are not mutually exclusive, of course; it is precisely the opposite that occurs in reading, as I experienced for the first time when I read Ursula K. Le Guin's children's classic: they are brought together. Reading is a different way of thinking.

That's how it was: literature was a hiding place for me, and at the same time a place where I became visible. And this, an outside place where what is inside becomes visible, is still what literature is to me. Literature and art, along with religion, are the only places I know of that are capable of establishing such an outside. Politics is inside, journalism is inside, scientific research and academic theses are inside, philosophy and social science, in fact every discipline I can think of is inside, and with the technological avalanche of recent years, tying together different parts of reality in a vast here and now, the reasons to write have not necessarily become more numerous, but they have definitely become more acute.

I would be lying, however, if I said that this is why I write. Obviously, I write for personal reasons, having to do with my private life, and these reasons are banal. I also write for existential reasons, concerning what it means to be, and these reasons are or can easily be perceived as being pretentious. And I write for social reasons, in that I am part of a linguistic and cultural community in which literary texts, be it poems, essays, short stories, plays, or novels, serve an important function, one that is increasingly downplayed or no longer fully acknowledged, but which as I see it is nevertheless essential.

The problem with an essay like this is that if I take on the first role and discuss my private reasons for writing, which have to do with wanting to be seen, wanting to be someone, with ambition and desire for success, I will come off as self-centered, shallow, and more than a little stupid, while if I focus on the other two roles, the existential side of writing and the function of writing in society, I will seem conceited, self-important, and perhaps also megalomaniac.

But as it happens, writing is precisely about disregarding how something seems in the eyes of others, it is precisely about freeing oneself from all kinds of judgments and from posturing and positioning. Writing is about making something accessible, allowing something to reveal itself.

Whatever it is that reveals itself may well be something already known, for there is hardly anything uncharted in the human psyche or in the world anymore, but it has to show itself unguardedly, with a kind of trust. It's like with the hedgehogs here in the garden: there are two of them, and if I want to see them as they are by themselves, I have to sit perfectly still in a chair and wait until dusk, when they emerge from their hiding place, and if I don't move then, they sometimes come all the way up to me, and I see not only their rotund, bristly bodies, their black eyes and black snouts, but also their way of being present in the world, their slow snuffling and shuffling, their cautiousness which at times turns into excitement and greed, even that of a slow nature. They don't see me, I see them.

The opposite can happen too, that crossing the yard in the darkness I inadvertently kick one of them so that it curls up into a ball and rolls along the flagstones.

The first method, sitting still and waiting for them to come out and become accessible to my gaze, is the novel's way of thinking, while the other, inadvertently stumbling over one of them in the dark and giving it a kick, is the logic of poems or short prose. In both cases it happens inadvertently — it doesn't matter whether it is the writer or what he is writing about that comes along inadvertently. Thoughts are the enemy of the inadvertent, for if one thinks about how something will seem to others, if one thinks about whether something is important or good enough, if one begins to calculate and to pretend, then it is no longer inadvertent and accessible as itself, but only as what we have made it into.

effect that certain connections emerged that I hadn't thought of or seen before. For example, the way we automatically arrange the things around us in hierarchies, assigning more value and significance to some things than to others, in an order so fixed that it never occurs to us to challenge it, as we do with established social and political orders and hierarchies, and yet the first kind of order is just as arbitrary. Or the connections between the body and its surroundings, how teeth resemble small stones and the mouth a cave, how the tongue is attached to the floor of the mouth like a mollusk to its shell, how the moist orifices of the body are to the surrounding skin as wetlands are to adjacent dry areas. Described thus, segmented into smaller parts, the material and objectlike aspect of the body becomes apparent and its similarity to other objects obvious, which for me, as I sat there writing, created a new connection to reality, in the sense that the trail running between me and reality took

As important as what form allows a writer to say is what it doesn't let him say. If one describes a particular town on a particular day, following the characters' thoughts practically minute by minute, all superstructures vanish, the arches of history and tradition disappear, leaving behind merely bits and fragments in between elements of the personal past and the ever-present impressions of the surroundings, the streetscape, the office, the beach, the bed. The difference between life as it really unfolds, always in the moment, and the overarching context we interpret it in but never live in will be revealed. If every chapter of this book is written differently, employing different strategies, for example one in the form of news journalism, another formed as a catechism, a third as a stream of consciousness, the relative nature of the way we understand ourselves and others will be emphasized, at the same time creating a sense that material life is something that goes on irrepressibly regardless of the forms of idea about. I am still not a fully fledged reader of Joyce, but precisely the way the moment dissolves connections, and how they are reestablished in different ways through the use of different styles, has been important to me over the past twenty years, if not directly in my own writing, then in my understanding of what it means to write about reality, and the extent to which one's worldview is inherent in the form. When I was nineteen and just beginning to write in earnest, I knew nothing about form – I knew what I liked, but not why I liked it – and I remember that mentally I set up two opposite extremes. On one side there was *Hunger* by Knut Hamsun, which I found fantastic, and on the other side, at the opposite end of the scale, there was Milan Kundera and his novels, perhaps especially *The Unbearable Lightness of Being*, which I felt an instinctive aversion to and didn't want to write about. (As if I could have written about it had I wanted to!) Now I understand what attracted me to Hamsun's form and put me off Kundera's, it had to do with closeness and presence — Hamsun follows his protagonist so closely that there is no plot, no construction of character, everything centers on him and what he sees, and it is as if Hamsun thereby describes the world as it comes into being, as it emerges for the main character. The world becomes the present, the world becomes the here and now, and this renders a dramatic storyline perfectly unnecessary, for the intensity of the present is such that everything becomes important and interesting. Kundera, on the other hand, uses an omniscient narrator who does as he pleases with his characters, placing them in various situations like a puppeteer, at a great distance from them, and the illusion of reality is constantly being broken. Kundera is a writer of ideas, a master of superstructure, and as an essayist he has no peer in contemporary letters. That I instinctively distanced myself from his form and literary strategies was partly because empathy was reportages protect us by confirming this.

The discrepancy between the reality I lived in and the literature I was writing at a certain point led me to throw in my cards and try something new. I wanted to get close to reality, and the genre with which I felt the greatest affinity at the time was the diary. What would happen if I combined the diary's closeness to the self and urge for reflection with the realist step-by-step novel? The rules I set myself now were exceptionally simple. I would write only about things that had actually happened, and I would write about them as I remembered them, without doing research or amending my memory to conform to other versions. I also had to write a certain number of pages every day, first five, later ten, and toward the end up to twenty. In that way I simply wouldn't have time to think, to plan or to calculate, I would have to go with whatever appeared on the screen in front of me. This method came about because I had set out to write about myself, and since we know more about ourselves than about any other subject, it seemed important to avoid the established versions and to seek instead the complexity that lies beneath our self-insight and self-image and which can be accessed only by not thinking about how our thoughts and feelings will seem to others, how it will look, who I am if I think and feel these things.

This form made it possible to see how closely interwoven the "I" is with the "we," how language, culture, and our collective notions course through us, how common even our most secret and solitary emotions are. I hadn't realized that before, nor did I expect to as I set out to write these books, for then my idea was to write about the most private of matters, that which was only my own, while what the form I had chosen enabled me to say turned out in the end to be the very opposite.

What I wanted with this book, which was eventually titled *My Struggle* and grew to six volumes, was to erode my own notions about the world, allowing whatever had been kept down by them to rise to the surface. The only way I could accomplish this was to abdicate as king of myself and let the literary, in other words writing and the forms of writing, lead the way.

That is also the method employed in writing this essay. I have written literary texts for thirty years, and for twenty of them I have done it full-time; in short, I have spent my entire adult life writing. This means that I know a great deal about what it is to write, and about why I do it. Yet despite this great knowledge, I have been sitting in front of my screen for three days, not knowing what to say — or rather, not knowing how to say it. And as soon as I got started, by writing that the simplicity of the question was treacherous, my pathway through the material took a certain direction, excluding all the other possible paths, so that only what I am writing now could be written. This is what became accessible, not all the rest. And perhaps even more important: I still don't know what lies ahead, what to say, where this essay is going.

This is so because I have to hit upon it inadvertently, or it has to hit upon me. It is one thing to know something, another to write about it, and often knowing stands in the way of writing. *Make it new,* Ezra Pound said — and is there any other way to do that than to let everything we know about something fall away and regard it from a position of defenselessness and unknowing?

~

The reason this text is so temporizing and eva-sive is of course that I don't quite know why I write, nor quite what writing is. I don't think anyone really does, to be honest, at least not in such a way that it can be fully accounted for. Whom is one addressing when one writes? Who am I in my writing, when form makes it seem foreign to me? How is it that all thoughts seem to vanish when one writes, even during the most intense and cerebral reflections? What are feelings in a text that consists of letters, black marks on a page?

On the other hand, I know — the way you just *know* something, for example roughly how much a stone will weigh in your hand (a certainty you become aware of if the stone turns out to be surprisingly light and made of papier-mâché) or that you love someone (in which case the answers to the question of why can never be as persuasive as the feeling) — both why I write and what writing is. The writer who has come closest to capturing it is Leo Tolstoy, in his great novel *War and Peace* from 1869, a book I love above all others, where it suddenly crops up in a scene set in the home of the Rostov family, whose daughter Natasha is being courted by Prince Andrew.

"After dinner Natasha, at Prince Andrew's request, went to the clavichord and began singing. Prince Andrew stood by a window talking to the ladies and listened to her. In the midst of a phrase he ceased speaking and suddenly felt tears choking him, a thing he had thought impossible for him. He looked at Natasha as she sang, and something new and joyful stirred in his soul. He felt happy and at the same time sad. He had absolutely nothing to weep about yet he was ready to weep. What about? His former love? The little princess? His disillusionments? . . . His hopes for the future? . . . Yes and no. The chief reason was a sudden, vivid sense of the terrible contrast between something great and illimitable within him, and that limited and material that he, and even she, was.

from an early age, they have the manual dexterity, the compositional skill and the sense of color required to produce a verisimilar image of reality. Van Gogh didn't have any of this, his figures were misshapen, his forms crooked and mean, his colors dark and lacking assurance, as if the paintbrush were his adversary, as if he were wading heavily through a swamp in the darkness while his contemporaries strolled across a sunlit meadow. He was on fire, driven by an intense will to communicate his inner world to the outer one, but the resistance was too great, the language he had access to was incapable of expressing it. But his will was as wild as it was blind, little by little the distance was whittled away until he produced his final paintings, painted only ten years after his first, and which are simple and rich and dizzyingly intense, full of an existential yearning which it is difficult to remain indifferent to. Van Gogh found a language, not for the illimitable within him, but for the longing of the illimitable to undulating shape against the gray cloud cover, while at the same time each separate jackdaw was clearly visible, flapping and screeching, with its hoarse *caw! caw! caw!* The feeling it gave me was one of shocklike joy at the simple fact that I was here, now, their contemporary. Joy that I existed, together with everything else in existence. When I see something like this, or when I look at a painting that evokes the same thing, I feel an urge to write, as if I have to find an outlet for it, find a form to express it in. Not the experience in itself, that means nothing, but the longing to be in the world which it gives rise to. Or to open the world. Yes, I write because I want to open the world. But when I sit down at my desk and switch on my computer, there is no way to get there, for language carries its own meaning, form carries its own meaning, and that which seemed so evident within me, so luminously clear and simple, and so near to me, to what I am, changes radically as soon as I begin to write, it is no longer near, it is no longer mine, and the meaning which language and form carry within them creates a distance, turns it into something else, at best a text which refers to an experience but does not itself contain it, at worst a text full of pretension written by a man unable to contain his emotions.

After I wrote this, I took a break and scrolled through the newspapers on my phone, and in one of them, the British daily *The Guardian*, there was a headline about one of my books. I never read reviews, not this one either, but the headline was enough to give me the general idea. It said "Sentimental, cliché, repetition." I had no time to shield myself, it felt like a slap in the face. I fetched the children from school, picked up some takeaway for dinner, slept for an hour to clear my mind of recent events so I could start writing afresh, flipped through the news on my phone again, this time only the

Norwegian news, thinking all was well, but there the review in England had already made the news, suddenly a headline flashed before me, "Knausgaard trashed by English critics: The book is a load of rubbish."

I mention it because it confirms how I myself view my writing, though I always push the thought aside, for if I make room for it, it paralyzes my writing, my self-confidence evaporates, and the only way to get it back is by writing something unquestionably good and thoroughly thought out, which in turn ensures that nothing can reveal itself, it can only be revealed. The experience also casts a different light on everything I wrote earlier. With what right do I mention Munch and van Gogh? How stupid I was to compare hedgehogs to writing novels! Why should anyone listen to me talking about why I write when what I write is worthless?

But I mention it also because the way my books are received, how they are interpreted and discussed in the public sphere, is of course a decisive part of my identity as a writer, whether the reception is positive or negative, and thus becomes not only one of several factors influencing what it is possible to write but also an important part of my motivation for writing. It isn't easy to talk about, for these are not honorable motives, on the contrary they are unworthy, even base – I'm thinking of revenge, of retaliation, of self-assertion, thirst for honor and rewards. But if I am to answer the question honestly, I have to include it.

The first time I thought of becoming a writer, and then began to write literary texts, I was eighteen years old. I no longer remember why I wanted to write, only that it seemed within reach, it didn't feel like such a big leap. I got a job as a teacher in a small village by the sea in the far north of Norway, I didn't know anyone there and would have plenty of time to write, that was the idea. It didn't turn out quite that way, but I wrote anyway, roughly one short story per month. Most dealt with childhood experiences, with my father as a domineering and dreaded figure, so one impulse to write must have been to work through those emotions.

But more important was what writing these texts made me into. Every time I wrote a new short story, I sent a copy to everyone I knew, and in the days that followed I waited for their responses. I wanted to be seen, and I wanted the recognition that came with being a writer, by becoming a writer I would show that I was someone special, that I was remarkable, that my work had a special significance, not like that of a junior high school teacher or a journalist but something more important, an author, an artist. I dreamed about it, not unlike the way I had formerly dreamed of becoming a soccer player or a pop star. It was as if I wasn't worth anything, and that I could be worth something only if I did something other people admired.

The year after, I was accepted into a creative writing program, they admitted only ten students per year, and when I entered the program I already considered myself a writer. Of course my hopes were crushed, everything I wrote was torn apart, and when I completed the program my confidence in myself as a writer was shattered. I continued to write anyway, squeezing out a short story or two per year, but nothing of what I wrote justified my will to write, for my short stories were not merely poor, they were practically pointless. Almost the only thing left was the will, something forced and immovable, like a carapace, and perhaps more than anything I kept it up because it would be so humiliating to have gone all out to become a writer, and then fail.

We knew it, people would say, he was just a conceited fool. And so I was: in my heart of hearts I knew that I was neither a writer nor an artist, I knew I didn't have what it takes. That I kept on trying anyway at times filled me with burning shame and despair, because it was so obviously a lie I told myself to maintain my sense of self. I knew I couldn't write, but I pretended to myself that I didn't know it—it was the same mechanism that once, when I was maybe twelve, had made me write down a poem by an English author in my diary and then pretend that I had written it. To myself, in my own diary!

And this was more or less the same thing: I wrote because I wanted to become a writer, I wanted to become a writer because I would then become someone in the eyes of others, at the same time that I knew for certain that I didn't have what it takes, and occasionally, in the clear light of shame, I admitted as much to myself.

Around that time I made a good friend, his name was Espen Stueland, and he wrote poetry. He was more than usually talented, and he was more than usually learned, he made his literary debut with a volume of poetry at the age of twenty-three. I realized that what he had was precisely what it took. He wasn't just a writer, he was a poet, which in my eyes was the ultimate achievement. When I met him he was nineteen, he read modernist poets whom I found completely hermetic, like Gunnar Ekelöf and Paul Celan, he read Beckett and Claude Simon, he had a picture of Edith Södergran on his wall, he found stuff in dumpsters that he brought to his bedsit and used, he played chess and he had a nervous energy which could turn into passionate involvement with whatever he happened to be reading.

The mere fact that he knew what he liked impressed me. I liked what I had been taught to like. I jostled for position, I knew that writing a thesis about *Ulysses* conferred status and that a little of Joyce's luster would rub off on me, so I did it; I knew that Tor Ulven and Ole

Robert Sunde were the two most sophisticated Norwegian authors, so accordingly I read them and liked their work, even though it didn't do much for me at the time. Espen, on the other hand, was a writer, he was the real thing, as uncompromising as he was thirsty for knowledge, and the difference between us was so great that spending time with him confirmed my conviction that I wasn't a writer at all, just a regular guy, at the same time that his fervent passion lit up my own reading too, lit up even my life as a reader.

Once we went to Prague together. I tried to see what he saw, experience what he experienced, and one afternoon when we were in a church and he sat down on a pew, I froze inwardly, for he remained seated for a long time with his eyes closed, and I felt certain that he was having a religious or spiritual experience, that something in there, in the same room I was in, had transported him into a state of ecstasy or deep contemplation. When we came out into read it and then suggested we take a walk together to talk about it. We walked up the hill toward the hospital outside town, past the large villa gardens there, I remember it well, it was cool and foggy, we had our hands in our pockets as we walked and he told me it wasn't good enough, he advised me to shelve the manuscript for good. After the initial shock, which hit me like an icy blast, I began to peck at him in my mind, what did he know, after all, he was just an elitist snob who wrote stuff even he couldn't understand, it was just words, and who the hell spent Friday evenings at home playing chess with themselves, anyway? But even as I was thinking these things, I knew that he was right, and that evening I followed his advice, I burned the manuscript in the fireplace.

I still wrote after that, though not much, completing maybe one short story the following year, and the first thirty pages of a new novel the year after that. The will to become a writer, to be someone who wrote, was now exclusively fueled by negative thinking, by my fear of losing face.

But there was something else there too. It wasn't merely a question of will, there was also a yearning. I didn't know what I yearned for — these were vague and inarticulate emotions, somewhere between the conscious and the subconscious strata of my mind — I knew only that it was something good. The things I wrote had no connection with this, and really no connection to myself, either, I wrote the way I thought literature was supposed to be, whether I happened to be modeling myself on Thomas Bernhard or the Swedish poet and playwright Stig Larsson. The text was an object, a construction, I could push it in one direction to say something about this, I could push it in another direction to say something about that. What mattered was that it looked like literature, or like my idea of what literature was. Nothing came back to me from these texts, they were wholly separate from me, like little monoliths, mindless and blind.

So where did the yearning come from? What was it I longed for, which I didn't know what was, but still knew about?

In these years I didn't read only difficult books that provided prestige, I also read books that I loved and could disappear into the way I had done as a child. Though I never reflected on it, these books were closer to me and the reality of my life than anything I wrote. Ask Burlefot, the young man in Agnar Mykle's novels *Lasso Round the Moon* and *The Song of the Red Ruby,* for example, seemed closer to me than I had ever felt any family member or friend of mine to be. In my social relations, all kinds of things represented a hindrance, hardly anything could be done or said, something always stood in the way, I was paralyzed by shame and low self-esteem combined with a high degree of self-reflection, I hardly spoke, and others hardly spoke to me. In Mykle's novels, on the other hand, almost nothing was forbidden, everything stood open, and although the protagonist, Ask Burlefot, was a fictitious character who didn't exist, the story about him unlocked things within me which would otherwise have remained dormant, as I read his experiences became my experiences, opening the way to emotions I hadn't known I could feel. Grief over the death of a younger brother, for instance: how was it possible that I was overcome by such a deep and lasting sense of loss, I who had never had a younger brother or experienced a death in the family or ever felt profound sorrow?

Of course, that kind of literary experience was what my childhood reading was all about, and this is why the step from reading to writing was such a short one when I turned eighteen: I wanted to be there, in that state of utter absorption where everything else vanished and you were, in a sense, out of the world. To read is to be the citizen of another country, in a parallel realm which every book is a door to. Feelings were generally a problem for me, I felt too easily and too much, and reading somehow provided relief from that, at the same time that it generated new and unfamiliar emotions. In my reading I was in a sense exploring and charting the boundless inner world that Tolstoy had written about. All of it fit within me, and my inner world expanded radically, while the world I was in remained unchanged.

Up until the age of nineteen, this is how I read, driven by the same motive: all I wanted was to be in that other world, on the other side. It didn't matter whether it was MacLean or Stendhal who took me there, Baroness Orczy or Ernest Hemingway. When I entered the creative writing program and later pursued literary studies at the university, this changed, for there I encountered a very different understanding of were to visualize a quality scale based on this view of literature, at one end, to the far left, we would place the novel narrated in such a way that it offers not the slightest hint of resistance, so that the reader glides through it like a hot knife through butter, what was once known as pulp fiction but is now sold in bookstores in hardcover editions, books in which everything is familiar, nothing is worth stopping to consider, nothing has value in itself. Moving toward the middle, we find what in Norway used to be called the "book club novel," it too with a broad appeal, containing few potentially exclusionary elements and plenty of recycled scenes and images, on to the acceptable novel, where cliché and crowd-pleasing have been excised but the underlying appeal to the reader is relatively intact, which brings us to other end of the scale, where resistance intensifies and narration, understood as those elements that serve to create an illusion of reality, diminishes, where the writing itself, how something is written, is given as much or more weight than what it describes, until we reach those books in which communication, the text's address to the reader, breaks down, in the kinds of extreme texts that were popular with poststructuralist literary critics, such as Joyce's *Finnegans Wake* and the poems of Mallarmé, perhaps because the "I" of these texts so manifestly doesn't control them, approaching the unconscious or perhaps the nonconscious, texts in which language seems to come close to the edge and perhaps even to cross it, into that which lies beyond language.

Presented like this, schematically and mechanistically, the quality scale seems rather ridiculous, and if there should be some truth in it anyway, quite revealing, for what is literature about if not the universally human, that which we all have in common, and what sustains this if not the act of addressing others?

But this is the value system I assimilated when I was at my most impressionable, in my early twenties, and it made a deep mark, so deep that I still, if driven into a corner, hold that the concept of literary quality denotes something that really exists, and that this is more or less what it looks like. The works of Celan and Mallarmé represent the pinnacle of literary expression. As a writer, on the other hand, I aspire to a different ideal: to one day be able to write something so essential and important that it speaks to all people, since it is true or relevant for everyone, irrespective of gender, class, or culture. These two ideals are diametrically opposed, it would seem that literary quality excludes reader address – why, how?

Once I watched a few episodes of *Game of Thrones*, it had been highly recommended to me, this was a time when people generally spoke very enthusiastically about HBO TV series, supposedly they were almost like novels. And the episodes I watched were good, the scenarios were believable, the actors highly skilled, the action grabbed your attention — as soon as one episode ended, I moved on to the next, I wanted to find out what happened, it was almost as if the plot hypnotized me, or like I was dreaming, for time passed imperceptibly and suddenly it was one o'clock in the morning. The whole time I watched I was full of emotion in response to what was happening on the screen. Joy, sorrow, excitement, fear — it all flowed through me. When I finally went to bed, however, I felt empty, in an unpleasant way, similar to how I felt after playing video games for hours on end in earlier years.

Why?

I think the reason is simple. What we seek in art is meaning. The meaningful carries an obligation. With obligation come consequences. If a child falls from a high tower, as happens in *Game of Thrones,* you might feel shock and a pang of something that resembles sorrow, which dissolves in the next instant, for the plot moves on and that the story is captivating is in fact the whole point. The child is forgotten. The feeling carries no obligation.

If a small child falls from a window and dies because its parents, who were having sex, weren't paying attention, as happens in Lars von Trier's film *Antichrist*, as a viewer you feel dread, horror at a fundamental level that won't let go of you, because the film doesn't let go of it, but instead examines the consequences in such a way that the woman's guilt activates your own sense of guilt, wrenches up something which until now had lain quietly within you, and if what is happening on the screen couldn't have happened in your own daily life, it can still happen in your emotional life, which the film constantly confronts and harries, so that it feels as if its archetypical or foreign images open up vast spaces within you, and in this way, for a time – the time it takes to watch the movie and perhaps for a few more days beyond that, and sometimes they can reopen years later, if something reminds you of the film's atmosphere or images — make you feel that your own person, your own life, is meaningful and important, connected with all that is important in life, and not only do you see it, at times you even reaffirm your commitment to it. That is what art does, it is essential. But it is still just an illusion, your emotions are engaged by a product of the imagination, the obligation isn't real, it is metaphorical.

If your own child dies, the feelings of grief and guilt are so powerful that they will always be there, there is no escaping them, you are bound to them and to what happened for the rest of your life. That feeling is impossible to convey to anyone else, it cannot be transmitted, cannot be sold, it addresses no one, it is yours alone until you die. That is what Mallarmé's long poem *A Tomb for Anatole* is about. It contains no sequence of events and hardly any address or communication, for grief is mute, turned toward darkness and emptiness, and so is the language of this poem. Reading it, there is no sense of drama, no burst of sorrow or sudden shock, the poem doesn't convey emotions, it is the emotion itself, its rending apart of meaning, coherence, language.

So at that time, you might say I was caught between two diametrically opposed experiences of what literature is and what it should do, one of which was based on empathy and identification, emotionally oriented and naïve, the other more cerebral, language-oriented, and sophisticated, though I never thought about it in these terms. All I knew was that the texts I wrote had no relevance. What I read did have relevance, but that seemed to occur in a different circuit, somehow, independently of what I wrote.

I read the prose poems of Francis Ponge, which had recently been translated from French into Norwegian. They dealt with objects, there were no people in them, it was as if the mute ourselves, which is so familiar and so taken for granted that we can't see it. Culture is a space where the world appears in ways that everyone who belongs within it agrees on. We agree that time is measured in years, months, weeks, days, hours, minutes, and seconds. We agree that weight is measured in kilograms and grams, we agree that distance is measured in kilometers, meters, and centimeters. We agree that all things are made up of something we call atoms, each of which in turn consists of a nucleus containing protons and neutrons orbited by electrons. We agree that all animals and plants belong to particular species, which in turn belong to particular genera, and that life arose in the ocean and then emerged onto land, and that the universe originated in a single point of unimaginable density which then expanded in what we call the big bang. This division of the external world seems so obvious to us that we think of it as reality itself, not just as ways we have of seeing and talking about reality or a conceptual framework through which the world appears.

Jorge Luis Borges is an author whose work operates in the to us invisible space between the world and its representation. He was obsessed with encyclopedias, which of course are alphabetical inventories of facts about reality. In his short story "Tlön, Uqbar, Orbis Tertius," one evening the protagonist, who is Borges himself, is sitting with his friend Adolfo Bioy Casares, also a real person, discussing literature. They talk about how one might write a novel in the first person and omit or distort facts, which would allow a few readers to sense a sinister or banal reality lying, as it were, behind the story. In the course of the conversation Bioy Casares refers to a country Borges has never heard of, namely Uqbar. Bioy Casares has read an article about Uqbar in an edition of the *Encyclopaedia Britannica,* but when they look it up in an edition kept in the house where they are staying, they find no mention of Uqbar. Later Borges comes across a volume of an encyclopedia that describes not only an unknown country but an unknown world: Tlön. It turns out that a secret society of scientists and academics, working across several generations and centuries, have described a fictitious planet down to the smallest detail, from its geography, biology, and history to its philosophy, religion, and psychology, from its architecture, art, and linguistics to its mythology and literature. Tlön's most salient feature is that the laws governing it are understood differently than are ours; the concept of causality, for instance, so central to our understanding of the world, is unknown there—"The perception of a cloud of smoke on the horizon and then of the burning field and then of the half-extinguished cigarette that produced the blaze is considered an example of association of ideas," Borges writes. Tlön's worldview is idealistic, and its inhabitants are incapable of understanding materialism, which is considered heretical. Borges frolics about among the more deviant ideas and notions of the world found in the history of philosophy, and I find myself wanting to quote his fantastic short story in its entirety, since it creates a reality that is completely different from our own and yet, up to a certain point, not impossible, since it deals, to a large extent, with differences in perception and not in physical reality, although the former gradually begins to affect the latter, and by the end, in the postscript to the short story, has also intervened in the reality in which Borges is writing at his desk: following the discovery of the literature about Tlön, its insights have slowly made their way into our world, both the language and the history of Tlön begin to replace language and history here, and objects from Tlön mysteriously appear, exhibiting properties that run counter to the laws of nature hitherto in force. "Almost immediately, reality yielded on more than one account," Borges writes. "The truth is that it longed to yield. Ten years ago any symmetry

Linné, Kant, Darwin, Mendel, Curie, Freud, Marx, Einstein, de Beauvoir, and other hegemonic writers have put forth in the past centuries, not only would our thinking change, so would reality itself: it would come to resemble the world as it appeared during the sixteenth century, interpreted in light of the Bible and its teachings, with a history dating back only a few thousand years, where the forces to which human beings were subjected belonged in the realm of the divine. The people who lived during that era also inhabited a space in which the world appeared in ways agreed on by all, and the question is whether their world was any less true than ours.

We believe in science, and our lives are dominated by its conception of the world, but even though the tenets of this faith, its descriptions of the principles of operation of physical reality, from the circulation of blood through our bodies to the disc-shaped and slowly dispersing galaxies, from the clouds of electrons circling atomic nuclei with unpredictable movements to the tiny mutations and displacements in biological matter which constitute our genes, can be measured and observed and placed within a larger, coherent, and logical system, and thus meet our requirements of truth, science provides no answers to ultimate questions, those we begin to ask ourselves as children, and which we perhaps seek to avoid in our daily lives but which are always there below the surface of our lives, and which occasionally, perhaps on a cold and clear autumn evening as you get out of your car and head up to the house and look up at the multitude of stars, you cannot stop yourself from formulating: What is the world? Where does it come from? What is the meaning of life? Where does this meaning come from? Who am I?

These questions, which are more important than all the rest, no one knows the answers to. That truth is beyond reach of the insights of science, whose movements in this respect perhaps most of all resemble those of a clown who as he bends down to pick up his hat ends up kicking it even farther away.

Both Borges and Foucault were interested in the space reality unfolds in, how it changes depending on our gaze upon it, and their efforts can be likened to a kind of fictional groundwork, since fiction too seeks to establish spaces in which the world comes into view. The implicit notion that literature might actually change the world, or our way of perceiving it, since to this way of thinking the world too is a fiction of sorts, was not something I thought about when I read either Borges or Foucault, and the insights they gave rise to were wholly absent from my writings from that time, they belonged to another circuit and soon sank in the mire of my subconscious. Nothing of what I read or experienced was I able to convert into literature, I was twenty-five years old and I wanted more than anything to be a writer, but I couldn't write. So I gave up. I had been working for a few years at an institution for the mentally impaired to earn money so I could write, now I realized that I couldn't do it anymore, and I went back to university, this time to study the history of art, and I gave it my all, I envisioned an academic career, perhaps in the end I could become a professor.

I made a new friend who also wrote, he too wanted to become a writer, and he too had had a manuscript accepted for publication when he was a mere stripling. His name was Tore Renberg, and I remember the day he told me that his book was coming out, it was spring, we were walking through the streets of Bergen below the university, and it felt like he was punching me in the stomach. For a few minutes everything went black, I was wild with envy and despair, I felt convinced that in some way or other this had sealed my fate; that I would never be able to write, never publish anything, now became an established fact.

That summer I began reading Marcel Proust's novel *In Search of Lost Time*. It had been translated into Norwegian for the first time a few years before, and when all the volumes had been published it was put on sale, so I could afford to buy the complete set. Every day I sat reading at an outdoor café in Bergen, and I was engrossed in it in the same way as when I read books as a child. The novel was like a place, and every morning I longed to be back in it. I didn't reflect on how it was written, I didn't consider the writer's intention, I just read and read and read.

Two years later, I was able to write. Tore was editing an anthology of new writers and asked me to contribute to it. I gave him a short story I had lying around. His editor, Geir Gulliksen, read it and invited me to his office, where he asked me whether I had written anything else. I hadn't, but the mere fact that he was interested was reason enough for me to stake everything on one card, quit my studies, move to Kristiansand, the town in southern Norway where I had lived as a teenager, and begin writing. I didn't know what I was going to write about, I had no idea for a book, I went to the local library and sat there, overheard a conversation, wrote it down and then let my protagonist come to Kristiansand and over-hear the same conversation. I made his diction more conservative than my own, not unlike the faintly French-accented, bookish language of the Norwegian Proust translation, and the distance this created, between him and me, or between the text and me, had the effect that my thoughts took on a slightly different hue when I wrote them down, and this slight for-eignness imperceptibly altered what followed, which suddenly seemed unfamiliar to me and beyond my control, at the same time that it was mine and came from me. It was just like reading, the feeling was exactly the same, I lost sight of myself and entered something at once unknown and familiar.

This was what I had been longing for. This was writing. To lose sight of yourself, and yet to use yourself, or that part of yourself that was beyond the control of your ego. And then to see something foreign appear on the page in front of you. Thoughts you had never had before, images you had never seen. It was the form that created them, for if what I put into the writing was my own and familiar to me, the form changed it, and that change demanded that I put something else into it, which in turn was transformed, so that even without moving I was moving away from myself. And that is exactly how it is to read, isn't it? Certainly, we open ourselves to another voice, which we turn into ourself, for when we read, what we feel are our own feelings, our own fear and enthusiasm, sorrow and joy, and when we reflect the reflections are our own, performed by our own self, but only as apprehended by the other, annexed by the other. Yes, I sometimes think, isn't it true that our self consists of what is foreign, of the other — for the language we think in isn't ours, it comes from outside us, it was there before we were born and will be there after we die, and the categories we think in are not ours, nor the conceptions nor the worldviews. All of this comes from the outside, and I think what happens when one writes is that the "I," which is really only a means to get a handle on things, a way of arranging everything one experiences, lets go so that the foreign and the others move closer to their own form, as represented by literature — as the system for transporting culture, thoughts, insights, feelings, images, notions from one person to the other — so that writing is as much about losing and giving back as it is about creating and taking.

Not that I was thinking of this as I sat there writing. It was like an avalanche, I wrote and wrote; when I went to sleep, I looked forward to waking up and continuing. It felt as if there were no boundaries in what I was writing, the text could go wherever it wanted, all I had to do was to follow its lead.

It led to a story about an infatuation and a relationship between the protagonist, who was twenty-six, and his thirteen-year-old pupil. It was a story about being shut up in one's own self and its endlessness, and it was about trying to break free from it, and about emotional immaturity and infantility, but also about innocence and purity, and the darkness that comes with the longing for innocence. And it was about the fear of authority.

That the novel I was writing had anything to do with Proust was completely lost on me. Now I can see that Proust's way of integrating action and reflection; his conception of metaphor, in which metaphor opens up parallel spaces in the text and creates a whole world around the protagonist; his nostalgia and his understanding of what memory is — all these were elements I used, believing them to be my own, and it was due to them that it became possible to write the novel.

Why had I written it?

I didn't know. Perhaps simply because I could.

When it was finished, I sent it to my brother. He read it, and the first thing he said when I spoke to him on the phone was, "Dad is going to sue you."

Then, one morning a few weeks later, when I had just received the proofs from the publisher in the mail and was about to go through them, the phone rang. It was my brother, he told me that Dad had died.

We traveled together to the house where he had died. I brought the manuscript with me in my suitcase, thinking I could go through the proofs in the evenings. But it was impossible, I just cried and cried, it felt like the bottom had been knocked out of me. The hatred I felt against my father, which was almost as old as myself, had vanished. I cried and cried, over him, over myself, over us. And my novel didn't mean a thing anymore. I suddenly understood that I had written it for him, for Dad. I had wanted him to see me. He never had. And now it was too late. He never got to read the novel, and he never knew that I had become a writer.

What happened in that house during that week changed me. And I knew I had to write about it. My first novel was published, it was a success, but when I set out to write a sequel, I could no longer write. I wanted to write about the death of a father and his son's relationship to him, but it was impossible. I wrote every day for four years, but it didn't work, nothing came, I was completely stuck. I had eight hundred pages of beginnings, none of them even came close to conveying what I had experienced, neither the personal things that had to do with Dad and me, nor what radiated from it, which had to do with the effect death has on our view of life. For after seeing my father lying there on the metal table in the chapel, I became aware of the world's materiality, the physical and material aspect of all things, including the people around me, who now emerged into view as bodies, physiology, biology, and that view has never left me, it is always there, just beneath social existence.

I tried to write short texts about things in the material world, strongly inspired by Francis Ponge, with the difference that among the real animals, objects, and people there would gradually appear things and people who didn't exist, slowly and imperceptibly another reality would impose itself, until it had taken over everything and everything belonged to it.

I wrote down several hundred words which I was fascinated by, including many denoting body parts, such as lungs, but when I sat there staring at the word and tried to write about it, nothing came, I had nothing to say about it, and I ended up abandoning that project too.

In those years I had a poster on the wall in front of me, from an exhibition by the film example turn to Tolstoy's novel *War and Peace*. I have read it twice, and both times I have been sucked into it, as happens only with the greatest of novels, when you invest more and deeper emotions into what you are reading than you do in your own life, and at times may find yourself yearning for the spaces opened up by the novel, even longing for its characters. The many moves, from country estates to towns, from society balls to battlefields, and the shifts between the various characters, who develop in accordance with their individual experiences and are therefore continually meeting in new ways, intertwining with and disengaging from one another, without ever standing alone, but also without ever realizing that this is so, since only we, the author and the reader, have access to every character's perspective. Turgenev's *Sketches from a Hunter's Album,* which sprang from the same time and culture, has almost nothing of what makes *War and Peace* a great novel. No action, no intrigue, no plot, no great beyond themselves, they are not part of a larger chain of events, and they stand open to everything — except the moment and the place. And that moment and place are the locus of our experience of the world. This ultimate authenticity, this presence in and of the world, is partially sacrificed by the novel in favor of form, which makes it possible to convey crucial insights into relationships in particular, but also into courses of events, psychological patterns, and social structures. That must be why it felt almost like a shock to read Turgenev after Tolstoy, it brought you so much closer to the landscape, the people, the culture, because that's where you were going and nowhere else: to that particular barn on that particular evening, for instance, and that must also be why I didn't believe in what I was writing when I tried to tell what happened in the form of a novel. I didn't want to write about the relationship between a father and a son, I wanted to write about Dad and me. I didn't want to write about a house where a grown man lived with his mother, like a variation on a theme from Ibsen's *Ghosts*, I wanted to write about that very house, and about the concrete reality within it.

I didn't know this during all those years I sat there trying, for me all writing is blind and intuitive, it either works or it doesn't, and any explanation of why a novel turned out the way it did will always be an ex post facto rationalization. Whatever works will force its way out in the end, as if by itself. So when, after ten years of trying and failing, I one day wrote a few pages about something that had happened to me, and which I felt so ashamed about that I had never told it to a single person, and did so in my own name, I didn't know why I was doing it, and I didn't at first see any connection with the novel I was trying to write, it was just something I did. I sent it to my editor, he called it "manically confessional," and I got the impression that he was taken aback, for it was pretty intense, and in literary terms rather poor. But it had something, both he and I could see that.

What was it?

First and foremost, freedom. For if I took this path, if I just wrote things down exactly the way I had experienced them, in my own name, it was as if all my worries about style, form, literary means, characterization, tone of voice, distance, all this vanished at a stroke, as if the literary side of it suddenly became mere make-believe, and superfluous: I could simply write. But it wasn't just this sudden freedom which lent it force, it was also that there was something unheard-of about it, that it was in a sense forbidden.

I was a novelist, I wrote novels, and if I used something from my own life, it had to be camouflaged, a part of the fiction. To renounce this was not among the possibilities open to me as a writer. For then it would no longer be literature.